Last Frontiers For Mankind
Defeating the
DESERTS

Evans

Evans Brothers Limited

CONTENTS

Introduction		**3**
Chapter 1	**Contrasts in the Desert**	**4**
Chapter 2	**Deserts of the World**	**6**
	Location of Deserts	
	Climates of Hot and Cold Deserts	
	Desert Landscapes	
	Vegetation and Pests	
Chapter 3	**The Deserts Advance**	**16**
	Desertification	
	Refugees	
Chapter 4	**People Advance**	**26**
	Emergency Action	
	Resettlement	
	Reclaiming the Desert	
	Farming the Desert	
Chapter 5	**The Future for People in Deserts**	**34**
	How Many People?	
	Water Management	
	Sun Power	
	Tourism and Mining	
Conclusions		**42**
Glossary		**44**
Further Reading		**44**
Index		**45**

INTRODUCTION

The main theme of **Last Frontiers for Mankind** is that the pressure we place on particular environments has thrown them all into a state of crisis. The nature of the crisis varies from place to place but there is always one common feature of crisis: crisis presents us with both danger and opportunity. Nowhere is this feature more obvious than in the world's deserts.

At the time of writing the world is watching the tragic events at the margins of the Sahara Desert. The sheer size of the crisis is scarcely understood. In human terms it is the greatest disaster the world has suffered since the Second World War.

Yet at the same time an opportunity is emerging even there. The world is not **just** watching this time: the degree of involvement, the amount of help offered is enormous. Much more will be needed in the next 20 years but there is already a growing sense of the desert world being a part of everybody's world.

Our understanding of desert environments is steadily increasing. New developments in agricultural and irrigation technologies are offering fresh opportunities to develop the deserts. But we are also learning to be much more cautious in pushing back the desert frontiers.

The deserts reflect very accurately the idea that crisis is both danger and opportunity. Desert is both drought and sunlight, empty land and overcrowded land, poor land and rich land. While some desert states are becoming poorer at a faster rate than most other poor countries, other desert states have become enormously wealthy. These contrasts are all considered in this book.

CHAPTER ONE

CONTRASTS IN THE DESERT

The name desert used to mean a place with no people. It is a deserted place. Only later has the name come to mean places that are very hot and dry.

Deserts cover almost a quarter of the world's lands but only 5 per cent of the world's people live in them. Most of these people live at the desert edges or at oases in the deserts.

People who live at the edge of the desert also live on the edge of survival. These people are brave and strong. But if the rains fail for a few years then the people suffer drought, famine, disease and death. In the years when the rains do come and the wells are full, there is plenty of grazing for the animals and food for the people.

Because desert environments can change so quickly they are often in crisis. For example, much of Ethiopia is in crisis now. But crisis means danger and opportunity. Crisis shows people the danger (problem) that faces them. The crisis can also show how to deal with it (opportunity). **This is the main theme in this book.**

The two photographs on pages 4 and 5 show this main theme. One oasis has been developed as an opportunity. The other has been lost because the problems of moving sand were not dealt with properly.

The second theme in this book is the problem of overpopulation. Overpopulation means that there are too many people or animals living in a particular place for that

The Timia Oasis, Niger. This is a small oasis surrounded by desert. High hills can be seen in the distance. At oases like this date palms are grown. There may be a small area of crops and water for animals as well as people.

place to support. It may not need many people to make a desert overpopulated. This second theme is discussed mainly for areas at the edge of the Sahara Desert. There are two reasons for this. First, it is there that desert peoples are suffering most. Second, the lessons being learned there can be used to help people in all other deserts.

The third theme is that desert lands are places of great contrasts. They include some of the richest and some of the poorest countries in the world. Some of the richest and poorest people live in them. Oil-rich sheiks earn a million pounds a day (2 million dollars) and the poorest peasants earn £100 ($200) a year.

Deserts include the hottest places on the earth's surface. But in some of these places people have died of the cold at night. Deserts are also the driest places on earth but may suffer from periods of severe flooding.

The fourth theme is that desert environ-ments are delicately balanced. They can easily be destroyed. Almost every way of helping the desert peoples could also very easily destroy their homelands. For example, some ways of bringing water to the soil to grow crops are also the ways of destroying the soil. Then nothing will grow there.

Desert lands are truly the lands of danger and opportunity.

Key words

oases – more than one oasis. An oasis is a place in the desert where water is regularly available.
environment – what a place is like and how the people live in it. People can change an environment; for example, by digging a well and making an oasis.
theme – a main idea.
contrasts – showing clear differences.

An oasis in Ismailia covered by shifting dunes. This oasis was a place where desert people had dug wells, planted date palms and grown crops. It was a meeting and resting place for travellers. Now it is destroyed by sand-dunes moving over it. Because the dunes were not fixed properly (see page 30) they have destroyed this important oasis. This oasis may be lost for many years, perhaps for ever.

CHAPTER TWO

DESERTS OF THE WORLD

LOCATION OF DESERTS

The map on this page shows the location of the main desert areas of the world.

There are four ways of reading this map that help us to understand more about deserts.

1 Each desert has a middle part that is **true** desert. It is hot and arid there. This arid centre is surrounded on most sides by **semi-desert** areas that have a little more rainfall. (See the graphs on page 9.) Most desert people live in semi-deserts.

2 We can then divide the deserts into two groups according to their distance from the Equator.

The first group can be named Tropical Latitude Deserts. They are on or near the Tropic of Cancer or the Tropic of Capricorn. For example, the Namib Desert lies on the Tropic of Capricorn, and the Sahara Desert lies on the Tropic of Cancer.

The second group is the deserts of Asia. They are sometimes named Mid-latitude Deserts. The Gobi Desert is an example. These deserts are also generally higher above sea level than most other deserts.

3 We can next read the map by seeing how far away deserts are from a coast. If we read the map this way we can see there are three groups of deserts:
   a coastal deserts, e.g. the Atacama Desert in South America.
   b inland or continental deserts, e.g. the Takia Makan Desert.
   c deserts so large they are coastal **and** continental. The best example is the Sahara Desert which stretches right across Africa and joins with the Arabian Desert. The Australian Desert is both coastal and continental.

4 The map key gives other information that divides the deserts into two groups. The groups are **hot** deserts like the Sahara Desert, and **cold** deserts like the Gobi Desert.

The main difference between these two groups is that cold deserts have at least one winter month with an average temperature below 6°C (43°F). Parts of cold deserts suffer severe frosts in winter. In summer their climate is much more like that of the hot deserts. These differences are clearly shown by the climate graphs on page 9.

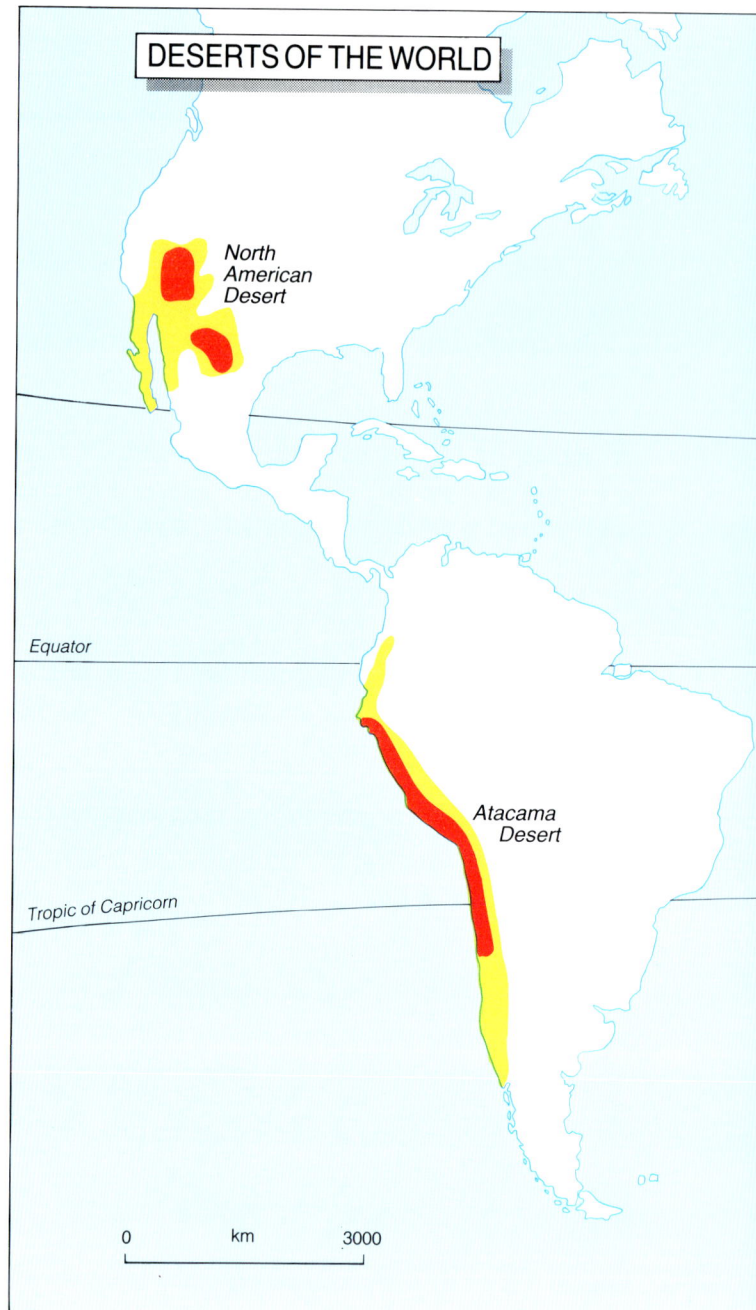

DESERTS OF THE WORLD

North American Desert

Equator

Atacama Desert

Tropic of Capricorn

0   km   3000

Takia
Makan
Desert

Turkistan
Desert

Gobi
Desert

U

M

Iranian
Desert

Tropic of Cancer

S a h a r a
D e s e r t

A

Arabian
Desert

Thar Desert

Somali
Desert

Kalahari
Desert

Australian
Desert

Namib
Desert

Climate Stations (see page 9)

Cold Deserts

desert

A   Aswan

The Gobi Desert

semi-desert

M   Mosul

The Takia Makan Desert

The Turkistan Desert

U   Ulaanbaatar

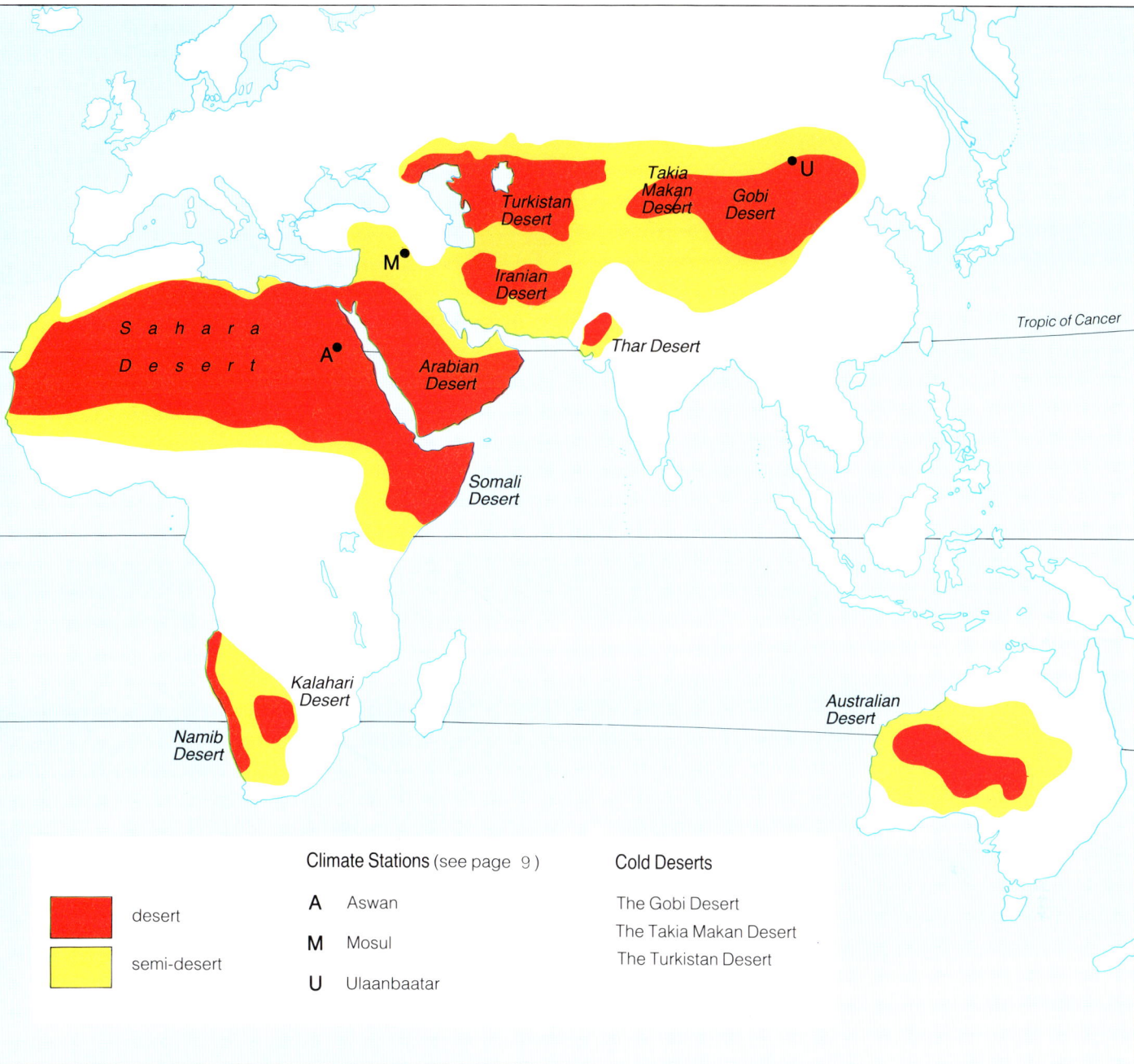

Reading the map in these four ways helps us to understand a little more about deserts. We can also name them properly. For example, the Australian Desert is a Tropical Latitude Continental Hot Desert with West Coast Margin. The Turkistan Desert is a Mid-latitude Continental Cold Desert.

Try describing some of the other deserts in this way. Which are the hardest to name clearly?

Key words

location – where a place is.
arid – dry, parched.
latitude – distance of a place from the Equator. This is usually measured in degrees. For example, the Tropic of Cancer is 22½° North.
mid-latitude – midway between the Equator and a Pole.
continental – middle part of a large body of land, e.g. middle Australia.

Salt Caravan Camels resting in the Danakil Depression, Ethiopia. This picture shows the brilliance of the sunlight. It also gives some idea of the heat. There is no shade and the camels must rest in the full glare of the sun. The salt they carry has been produced by evaporation of water in the intense heat. The salt is left behind when the water is evaporated away.

CLIMATES OF HOT AND COLD DESERTS

Deserts are lands with few people. They are also hot and arid. Temperatures are measured in the shade.

Temperatures in Hot Deserts

All the hot deserts of the world record very high temperatures especially in the summer months. The climate graph for Aswan, Egypt shows the temperature curve for the year (see graph A, page 9). For most of the year average temperatures are well above 20°C (68°F).

In the Danakil Depression, Ethiopia, the highest average annual temperatures are almost 35°C (95°F). That is the **average** over the year.

If temperatures measured in the shade are high those measured in sunlight are amazing. In some places in the eastern Sahara Desert they reach 85°C (185°F). It is not surprising that the camels shown in the photograph are resting through the heat of the day.

Temperatures in Cold Deserts

Temperatures are much lower here. This explains the name of these deserts. The graph for Ulaanbaatar in the Gobi Desert shows this (see graph B, page 9). The winters are bitterly cold. The summers are fairly hot. But note that the hottest months are only slightly hotter than the coolest at Aswan (see graph A, page 9).

The differences between the temperature graphs for Aswan, Tropical Latitude Desert

GRAPH A: ASWAN
tropical latitude
hot desert

GRAPH B: ULAANBAATAR
continental mid-latitude
cold desert

GRAPH C: MOSUL
semi-desert

N.B. The positions of these places are shown on the map on page 7.

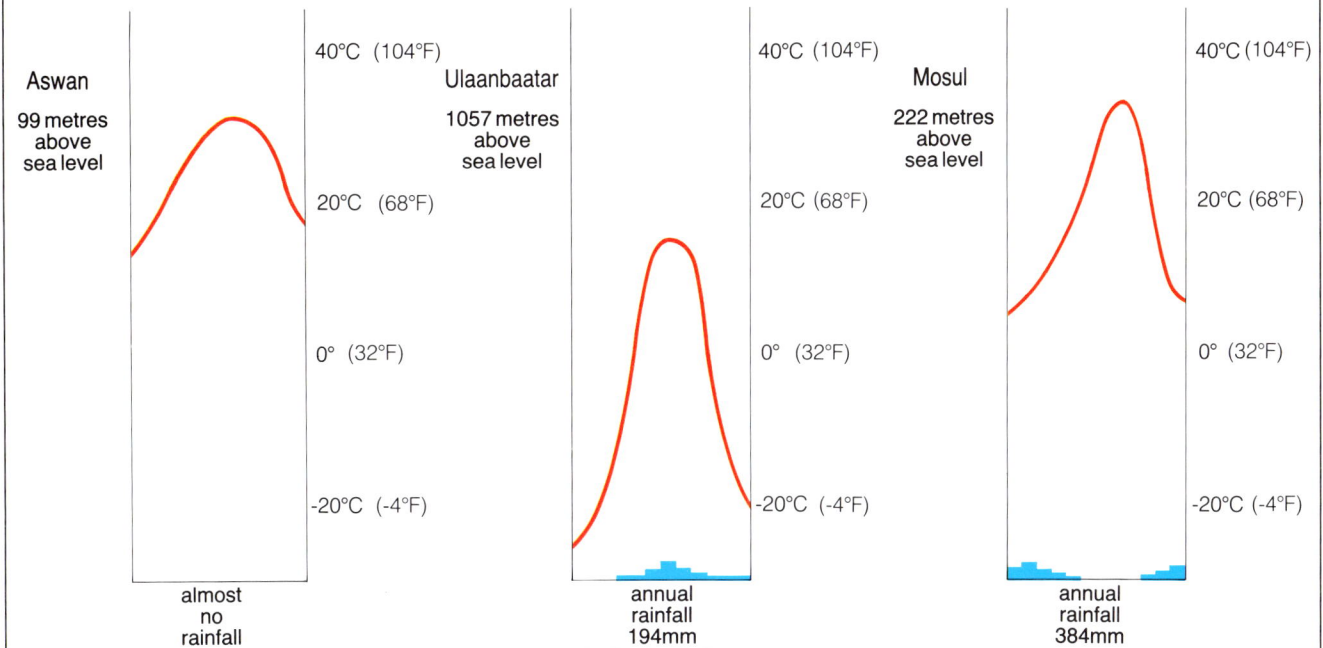

Aswan

99 metres
above
sea level

40°C (104°F)

20°C (68°F)

0° (32°F)

-20°C (-4°F)

almost
no
rainfall

Ulaanbaatar

1057 metres
above
sea level

40°C (104°F)

20°C (68°F)

0° (32°F)

-20°C (-4°F)

annual
rainfall
194mm

Mosul

222 metres
above
sea level

40°C (104°F)

20°C (68°F)

0° (32°F)

-20°C (-4°F)

annual
rainfall
384mm

(see graph A) and Ulaanbaatar, Mid-latitude Continental Cold Desert (see graph B) are explained by three facts:

1 Ulaanbaatar is in a continental desert. It is **ten times further** from the warming influences of the sea than is Aswan.
2 It is **ten times higher** above sea level than Aswan.
3 It is **twice as far** from the Equator. Aswan is at 24°N. Ulaanbaatar is at 48°N. Their positions are shown on the map on page 7.

Sunshine Hours

Another measure of heat is how many hours of sunshine a place has. This is called sunshine hours. In some parts of the eastern Sahara Desert there are more than 4000 sunshine hours a year. This is an average of more than ten hours per day. Most of the cold deserts record less than half this amount despite their hot summers.

Desert lands which have cloudless skies in the day become very hot indeed. But because the nights are also cloudless the land cools down very quickly. Some hot deserts may even have frost at night. The differences between temperatures for the hottest part of the day and the coldest part of the night can be very great indeed. This difference is the **daily range of temperature.** In some hot desert areas it is bigger than the difference between summer and winter. It could be said that night is the winter of the deserts.

Key words

average – the result of adding up some figures and dividing the answer by the number of figures. For example, the average temperature of 80°C (176°F), 40°C (104°F) and 30°C (86°F) is 50°C (122°F). Note that the average temperature did not actually occur.
annual average temperature – this is the average temperature worked out for the whole year.
evaporation – turn a liquid into a gas, in this case turning water into water vapour. When this is done salts may be left behind. Evaporating sea water produces large amounts of salt which are sent to other places.

Rainfall in Deserts

Deserts are arid lands. It is often the amount of rainfall received that decides the way of life of the desert people.

Deserts are areas of **low rainfall.** The average annual total rainfall is less than 250mm. At Aswan (see graph A, page 9) so little rain falls it is not even drawn on the graph. Life here depends on well water and irrigation from the River Nile.

The second feature of desert rainfall is that it is **unreliable.** It is this that explains some of the disasters suffered by desert peoples.

Rainfall can be unreliable in several ways:

1 Over a period of years rainfall can be less than expected for year after year. This creates drought conditions. This is shown in the graphs on page 21.
2 Rainfall is also unreliable during each year. For example, the rains may come early or late or not at all in the three month rainy season. Or the rains may come in short violent storms. A desert place may receive all of a year's rain in one day. It will be impossible to store much of this water for crops in their growing season.

In places experiencing these problems desert conditions may spread even though the total average rainfall is more than 250mm per year. Once again the average may not mean very much. The Sahel in Africa has suffered very badly from drought and unreliability of rain. (See the map on this page. This is discussed in chapter 3.)

Another major problem in all deserts, including cold deserts, is that much of the rain that does fall is lost by evaporation. If a rainstorm is followed by several hot, cloudless days all the rain held on the ground will quickly evaporate.

Sometimes it is so hot that the rain evaporates **before** it even reaches the ground. It can be seen leaving the clouds but it does not reach the ground. This is named **phantom rain.**

In some semi-desert areas the rainfall is more than 250mm a year. The graph for Mosul in Iraq shows this (see graph C, page 9). (It is helpful to compare this graph with those for Aswan and Ulaanbaatar.)

The average annual rainfall total at Mosul is 384mm. This is far more than at Aswan and twice as much as at Ulaanbaatar. But there is another advantage when compared with Ulaanbaatar. At Mosul the rainfall is **winter rain.** It falls when the effects of evaporation are least. At Ulaanbaatar much of the **summer rain** is lost by evaporation.

Unfortunately, what appears so favour-

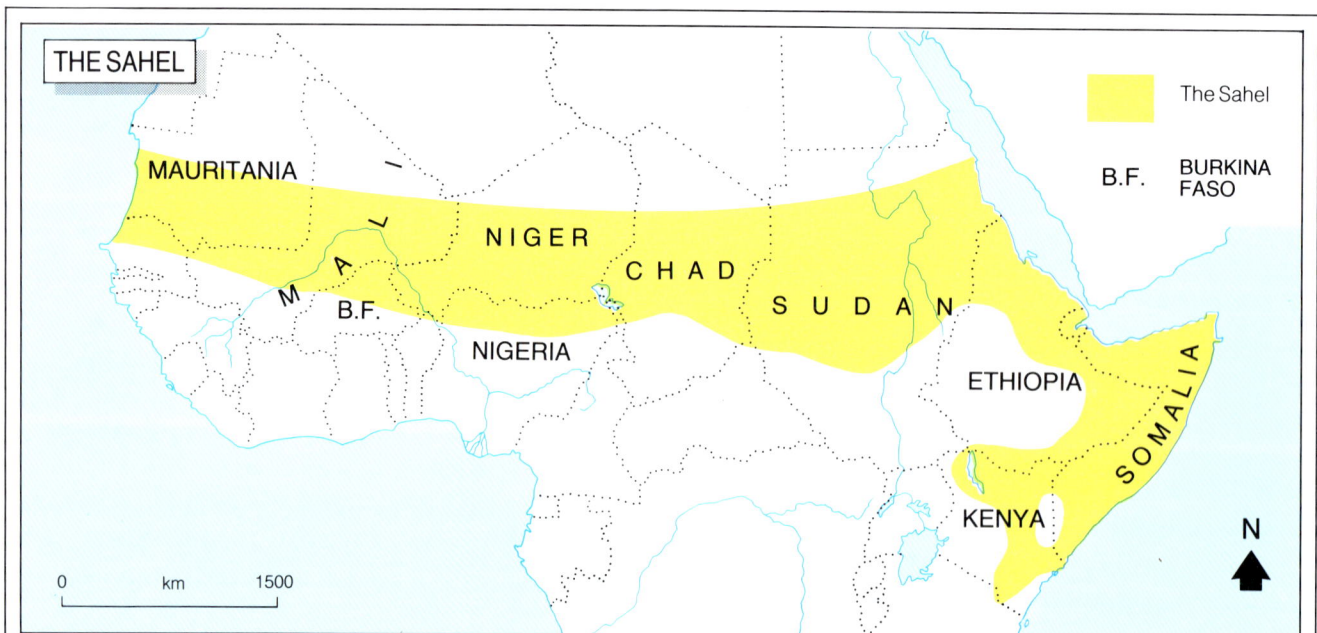

The Sahel. This large area of Africa crosses several states. This is the area affected by severe drought. (See chapter 3.) It lies on the south side of the Sahara Desert.

Namib Desert, Southwest Africa. An aerial view of sand dunes in the fog.

able at Mosul does not give a true picture. At Mosul the rainfall is as unreliable as in most other places. Several years may pass with a total each year of much less than 384mm of rainfall. While conditions may never be as bad as in the heart of a desert, semi-desert areas are also places of difficulty for the people.

Why Deserts are Dry

Deserts are dry for different reasons. It depends very much on their position. The map on page 6 shows that the deserts can be grouped according to position.

Continental deserts are just too far away from the sea for rain-bearing winds to reach them very often. Also when winds do blow they often blow out of the desert as a dry wind. These deserts include all the cold deserts of Asia, much of the Sahara Desert, the Kalahari Desert and the Australian Desert.

Other deserts are dry because mountain ranges prevent rain-bearing winds from reaching the deserts. The mountains make a rain shadow area. Much of the North American Desert is in the rain shadow of the Coast Ranges and the Rocky Mountains. Other places affected in this way include parts of the northwest Sahara Desert and northern Atacama Desert.

The deserts with the most interesting position are the Atacama and Namib Deserts. They are on coasts where winds do sometimes blow from the sea. Yet both areas are hot deserts. The reason for this is that the winds blow over cold ocean currents before they reach the land. The air is cooled down. Cool air can carry very much less water vapour than warm air. As a result when the air reaches the land it may only contain enough water to make fog but not enough to make rain. The photograph on this page shows a dune landscape in the Namib Desert in fog.

Most deserts are dry not just for one of these reasons but for several reasons together.

Barren scene in the Hoggar Mountains, Algeria. Two different desert landscapes are seen here. There is a large area of stony desert or reg. This area is barren. In the distance can be seen an area of high, bare mountains forming another kind of desert landscape.

DESERT LANDSCAPES

Deserts are barren places. They are barren because they are arid.

The photograph on this page is of a stone desert or **reg.** This kind of barren landscape is found in many deserts. No plants grow here.

In the distance can be seen a second kind of desert landscape. It is a place of **high, bare mountains** from which all the soils have been washed away. A similar landscape is shown in the photograph on page 13.

A third kind of desert landscape is known as **hamada.** It is a roughly level area of bare rock. All the sand has been swept off it by the wind leaving great polished slabs of rock exposed to the sun. Nothing grows there.

The fourth and best known desert landscape is the sand desert or **erg.** About one third of the desert lands are like this. The photograph on page 11 and the large cover photograph show exactly what they are like. This kind of landscape is sometimes named a sand sea. This is a good name for two reasons. First, the dunes are often pushed into wave-like shapes by the wind. This can be seen in the photograph on page 11. The second reason is that the wind causes the dunes to move across the country like moving waves. The movement may be very slow but the dunes will bury and smother whatever is in their path.

This is why it is important to fix dunes in position by planting them with grasses and trees before crops are grown. This is shown in the photographs on pages 30 and 31. The damage moving dunes can cause is shown on page 5.

In all four of these desert landscapes there is almost no plant life to bind soils or sands together. This is why erosion by the **wind** so easily moves material about; for example, sweeping sands clear of the hamada desert. In other places the wind whips up sand and dust-storms. (See the photograph on page 19.)

The loose nature of desert surfaces also explains why **rain** can have such a powerful effect on desert landscapes. Although rain rarely falls in deserts it usually falls as powerful rainstorms. These storms fall directly onto the loose sands and soils. They are ripped away and carried to other places where they are dumped. (See the photograph on page 22.)

In mountainous country the rain water, loaded with sand and pebbles, rushes down the dried up valleys or **wadis.** The wadis will be cut deeper and all the loose material swept out into the plains. The photograph on this page of Wadi Kelt in Israel is an example of this kind of erosion. In the front of the picture the flat floor and smoothed rocks show the effect of this kind of attack.

Desert landscapes are attacked in other ways as well. Because the daily range of temperature is so great (see page 9) rocks are always being expanded and then contracted by the heat. This splits open the surface of boulders into fine cracks. If any moisture gets into the cracks chemical changes take place. For example, any iron in the rock will begin to rust. This causes the rocks to peel and crack like onions. Boulders become rounded as the corners are split off. Small pieces of rock are broken down into smaller pebbles. The photograph of the reg on the facing page shows some of the effects of this kind of **chemical weathering.** As boulders become smaller they are more easily moved around by the rare rainstorms.

The barren desert landscapes of the world show slow changes as they are attacked by the weather. The one exception to this is that violent rainstorms can cause big changes in only a few hours.

Key words

landscape – the appearance of a place, the scenery.
barren – bare, not fertile.
arid – dry, parched. (See also page 6.)
erosion – the breakdown and removal of rocks. For example, pebbles being broken down to sand grains and then blown away by the wind.
weathering – breakdown of rocks under attack from the weather. (We use the word erosion if the material is transported somewhere else.)

Wadi Kelt, Israel. This is a good example of a wadi. It has a flat floor and steep sides. Only after heavy rains will water rush down this wadi carrying away any sand or pebbles that have collected in it. Built across the wadi is a Roman Aqueduct about 2000 years old. It is now a ruin. How did the Romans build this aqueduct to allow flood waters to run down the wadi?

VEGETATION AND PESTS

Few plants can live in arid deserts. Outside the oases and croplands cared for by desert peoples there is very little vegetation.

The photograph on this page was taken in the North American Desert. Because so many films, especially cowboy films, have been made there people believe most deserts look like this. This is not so. Most deserts look like the scenery shown in the photographs on pages 11 and 12. What this photograph shows that **is** true in all deserts is that plants have to be specially adapted to survive the drought conditions. Plants that are adapted in this way are named **xerophytes.**

One of the main ways xerophytes are adapted is that their leaves are often small and waxy. This helps the plants retain water. Other plants, like the cacti in this photograph, are adapted to store water in their trunks. Large cacti may be up to 20 metres tall and store more than 5 tonnes of water in their bodies. Other plants develop very deep root systems. These burrow down for as much as 15 metres searching for moisture.

Almost all these xerophytic plants grow very slowly. Some can stay dormant for more than a year. A visitor to the desert might decide that most of the plants are dead. But as soon as rain does fall some plants grow new leaves, and many others burst into flower. Many cacti carry brilliant flowers for just a few weeks or days after rain.

Rain in deserts brings to life the second important group of plants. These are named **ephemeral plants.** Their seeds can survive in sands and in cracks in rocks for up to twenty years. Rain causes the seeds to germinate very quickly and then the desert bursts into wonderful displays of grasses and flowers. The desert may be carpeted with varieties of daisy and desert dandelion. This period of flowering may last for six to eight

North American Desert, Mexico. This view shows a variety of desert plants. Note also the exposed, dusty nature of the soil.

weeks. Then the flowers die away as quickly as they appeared. They will not be seen again until the next rains.

Many of these plants, like the crops grown by the desert peoples, are always in danger from different kinds of pests. These pests are either natural inhabitants of the desert and semi-desert or they have been introduced there by people.

Locusts are probably the best known natural pest. They breed in marshy areas outside the deserts. Then they collect in huge swarms and fly across country eating all the plants in their path. They are especially dangerous in North Africa, the Middle East and parts of India and Pakistan. Much has been done to control them by spraying the breeding grounds in the marshes. But new strains of locust have developed that are no longer killed by chemical sprays. In some places the problem is almost as serious now as it was forty years ago.

The best known pest introduced by people is probably the rabbit in Australia. Every kind of control has been tried there including poisons, deliberately encouraging disease, and dividing up the countryside with rabbit-proof fences.

But the animals causing the worst problems in several deserts are goats. These hardy animals are kept for their milk, meat and skins. In some areas they are the most important source of food for the people. But goats have very big appetites and will eat almost anything. Because they are kept in nomadic herds wandering the desert they are very difficult to control.

Desert Locust. Here is a desert locust which was caught on a millet leaf. It can eat several times its own weight in a day.

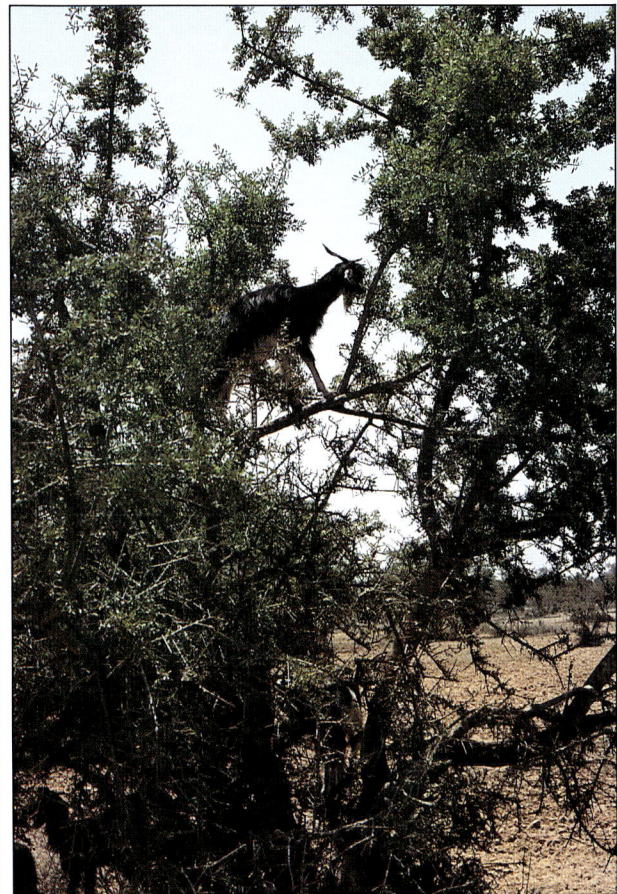

Goats strip trees at every height they can reach. It is not surprising that goats have been described as 'wingless locusts'. This photograph was taken in Morocco but similar things happen wherever goats can reach plants.

Key words

adapted – changed to suit a special condition, in this case drought.
xerophyte – a type of plant adapted to hot and dry climates.
dormant – as if in sleep.
ephemeral – lasting only a few days.
germinate – to put out shoots and buds.

CHAPTER THREE

THE DESERTS ADVANCE

When desert conditions spread into new areas the process is named **desertification**.

There are **three** main causes of desertification. They are:

1 desertification by people

2 desertification caused by climatic change

3 both causes together

1 DESERTIFICATION CAUSED BY PEOPLE

People may **destroy** the balance of their environment in a number of ways.

1 Overburning

In some savannah and semi-arid areas the land is cleared for farming by burning off the vegetation. Usually the burning is not controlled, and repeated burnings kill the trees as well as the undergrowth. (See the photograph on this page.) There is no longer a protective cover of vegetation. The soil is dried by the sun, it becomes loose and **friable,** and dust-bowl conditions are created. (See the photograph on page 19.)

Deliberate burning of savannah grassland south of the Sahara Desert. The desert has been spreading southward for most of this century.

Flood irrigation. In this view in Upper Egypt the fields at the bottom and right of the picture have already been destroyed by salting.

If flood irrigation continues to be used the other fields in the area will be affected in the same way. Nothing will grow in the soil to protect it from erosion.

2 Overcropping

After working the land until its fertility is exhausted people abandon it and move to new areas. The soil does not develop a full, new cover of vegetation because it is exhausted. Desertification may begin.

3 Deforestation

In many areas trees provide the main source of fuel and building material. When they are cut down (**deforestation**) the soil is no longer protected. The soil is swept away. Around a number of towns in Burkina Faso, Niger and Chad the land has been cleared of trees across areas 150 kilometres wide. Desert conditions are surrounding the towns. (See the photograph on page 20.)

4 Overgrazing

When people allow their animals to graze freely **overgrazing** may result. Of all the animals herded by people goats are probably the greediest grazers. (See the photograph on page 15.) They not only restrict plant growth by grazing the new green shoots as well as the leaves, they also eat the protec-

tive bark off the trees. Only the thorniest, most prickly of plants are left untouched. Once again the balance of the environment is disturbed and desertification begins.

5 Wrong methods of irrigation

In some areas flood irrigation has formed waterlogged soils. These soils become salt-saturated and nothing will grow. If the area is abandoned desertification might begin. The first stage of this process is shown in the photograph on this page.

Key words

friable – easily turned into a powder.
deforestation – clearing the trees from the land.
overgrazing — destruction of vegetation by putting too many animals on the land, or by allowing a few animals to stay in the same place for too long.
savannah – name for tropical grassland close to the edge of the desert.

Desertification may also be caused by people in other ways. People do not **protect** the balance of their environment.

Many groups living at the edge of the desert are traditionally nomadic or semi-nomadic. For example, they may practise the methods of shifting cultivation. This means that they move on to new lands when their old homelands no longer support them. As long as there were few people and plenty of empty lands this traditional way of life worked very well. But now it is beginning to fail as populations increase and the 'empty' lands fill up or are already lost to desert.

Scene at a watering hole. An Afar woman with her camel, goats and belongings, Danakil Desert, Ethiopia. Some of her possessions have been made from plant branches and fibres. The goats may kill the plants on which she depends.

Dust storm in the desert, Saudi Arabia.
Here the loose soil has been swept up by the wind and may be carried many hundreds of kilometres. Storms lifting to this height are of fine soil particles. Desert sand is rarely lifted above waist height.

People who do not stay in one place do not learn to protect the land.

1 As the soil becomes exhausted people do not add compost or fertilizer to the ground. They do not dig in plant remains from the previous crop.
2 They do not plant a protective screen of shrubs and trees as windbreaks, nor protect plants from their herds.
3 They do not control their grazing animals and they make no farming use of their manure. If manure is collected it is not dug into the soil to fertilize it. Instead it is dried in the sun and then used as a major source of fuel.
4 When the rainy season does come some communities do not know how to make best use of the water. The rains are allowed to flood the ground eroding and destroying the soil.

The most serious problem with desertification is that the people who cause it do not understand what is happening.

They lack the **education** they need in new farming methods. They lack the **education** they need to understand that the remaining habitable lands are filling with people, and that the destroyed lands will not recover by themselves. People may not understand that there is any need to change the old ways of tribe and family until they are starving in a refugee camp. It may be too late for the people to be saved. It is too late to save the lands that have been destroyed.

Look at the Afar woman in the photograph on page 18. If her children are educated to prevent the destruction of their environment what kinds of lessons will they have to learn?

2 DESERTIFICATION CAUSED BY CLIMATIC CHANGE

The climatic change that most contributes to desertification is repeated failure of the rains. (Desert climates are discussed more fully on pages 8–11.)

Areas like the one in the photograph on this page depend almost entirely on the rain falling directly onto the soil or being trapped

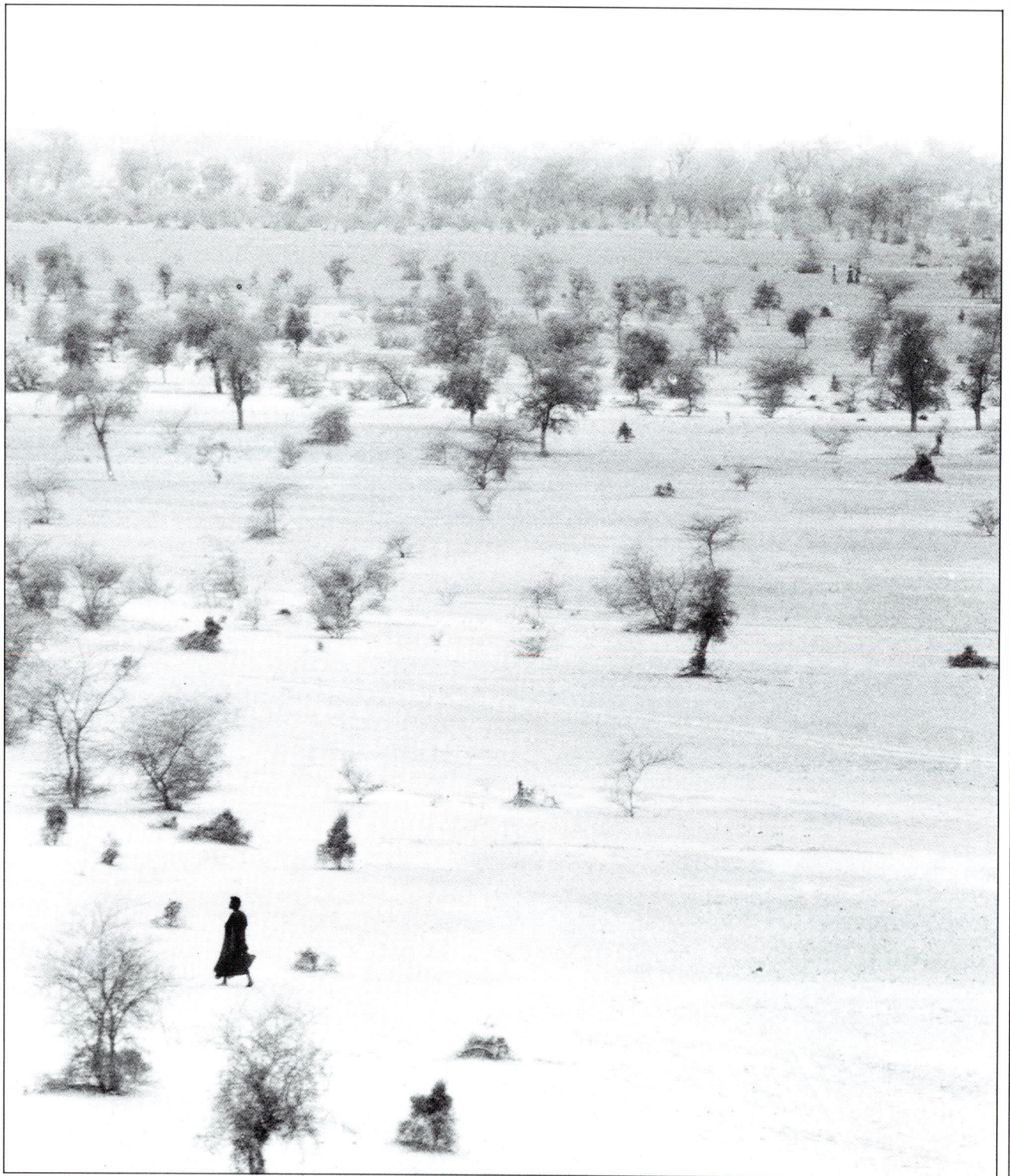

Desertification. This photograph was taken at Gorom-Gorom in Burkina Faso. Fifteen years earlier this area was thick with trees. When the woman walking to market was a girl she would have followed a pleasant winding path through woodlands.

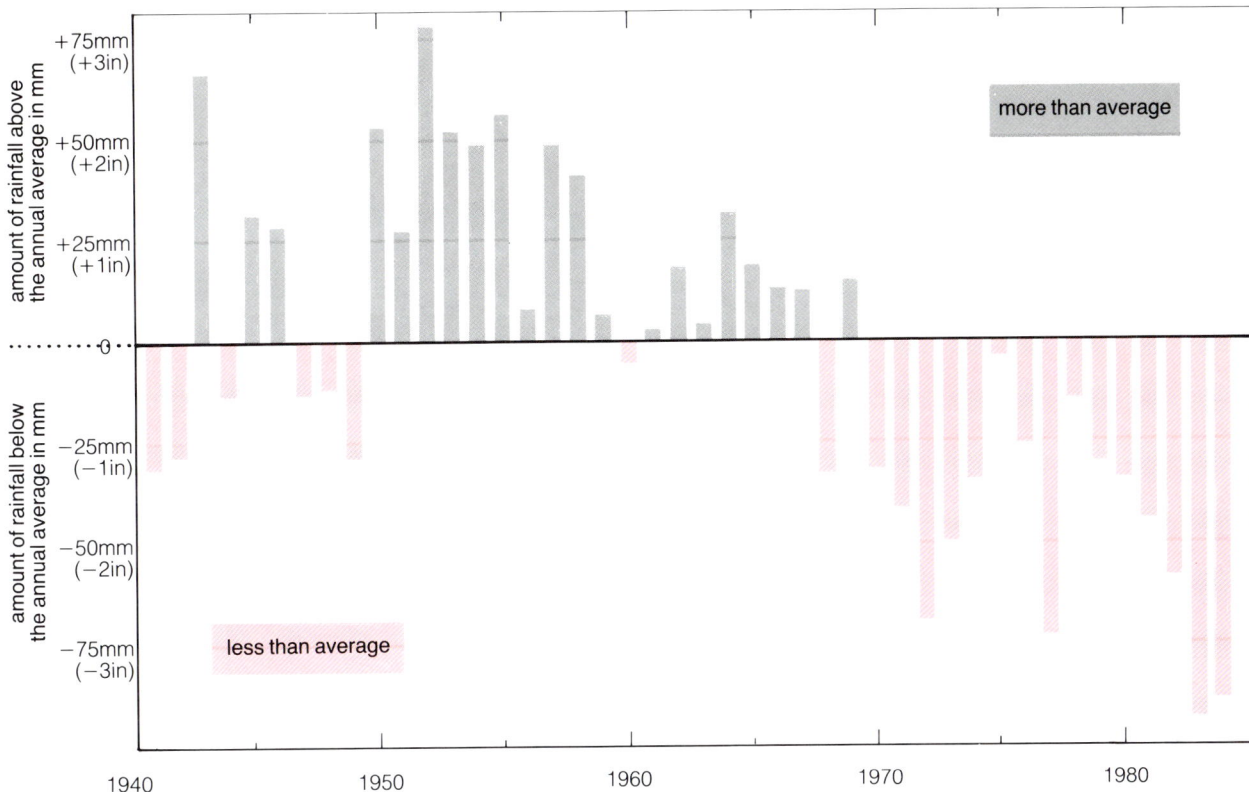

ANNUAL RAINFALL VARIATION:
WEST SAHEL 1940-1985

This is a graph of rainfall variation in the West Sahel from 1940 to 1985. It shows how total rainfall for each year was more than or less than the average annual rainfall for the whole period 1940–1985.

It shows that in wetter years the rainfall exceeded the average; in dry years it was less than the average annual rainfall.

Note that in the period 1940–1970 groups of dry years were followed by wetter years. But since 1970 that NEVER happened. Every year has had a rainfall total below the average annual rainfall.

in small basins and wells. If the rains fail for six or seven years in succession then the rain in the next year may just wash away what is left of the soil. The last hope of recovery is destroyed.

Failure of the rains leads to the most serious problems in areas far from rivers and dams. But even people living beside rivers begin to suffer if the rains fail too often.

The graph on this page shows how rainfall in the Sahel has changed in the last 45 years. Several years in which rainfall was above the average have been followed by years when the rainfall was below the average.

As a result drought conditions have become increasingly severe since 1970. None of the trees that grow in semi-desert conditions can survive more than seven years without rain. The combination of drought plus the death of the trees has resulted in the spread of desertification.

The other characteristic of rainfall in lands near the desert margin is its irregularity **within** each year. If this irregularity is extreme then desertification may begin even though the annual rainfall total is more than 250mm. For example, in a semi-arid region with annual rainfall of 350mm this total may appear to be enough to support the way of life of the people. But if half of that total falls in one afternoon in February and there is no more rain until November, this semi-arid area may begin to become an arid area. If this irregular pattern is repeated over several years then desertification may spread into the region.

3 DESERTIFICATION CAUSED BY PEOPLE AND BY CLIMATIC CHANGE

It is not always easy to decide **how much** of the desertification is due to failure of the rains or to poor farming methods. For example, in the area around Gorom-Gorom (see photograph on page 20) it is not at all clear if

deforestation has speeded up desertification started by climatic change. However, it is in the Sahel that these combined causes are generally the most obvious.

In the Sahel (see map on page 10) the desert is spreading southward. There is a link between increasing unreliability of rainfall and the effect of shifting agriculture. Areas where the land was originally cleared

Too much water. Storm over Etosha Pan, Southwest Africa. In this area heavy rainstorms have washed unprotected soils off the slopes and dumped them in the Etosha Pan. The soils then dry out and become increasingly salty. None of this can be used for farming.

Too little water. A farmer in Chad makes use of the last water in a well that may soon be dry.

by burning or deforestation are suffering desertification. In some of these places the effects of overgrazing have added to the disaster.

Scientists studying these effects are reporting that not only is desertification spreading it is also spreading **faster** each year.

To the east in Sudan and Ethiopia, the link between bad farming methods and decreased rainfall can be seen in several regions. There are also other complicating factors. In much of eastern Ethiopia farming has broken down because of civil war. In some places the war has lasted more than twenty-five years. Much of the land has been abandoned because of the fighting.

In these locations and others like them the people are caught in the tragic downward spiral shown in the diagram on this page.

Because of the terrible tragedies occurring in the Sahel it is natural to concentrate our attention, and the attention of the whole world, on what is happening there. But all the world's deserts may suffer the effects of climatic change and of bad farming methods.

In the Indian Desert of western India and

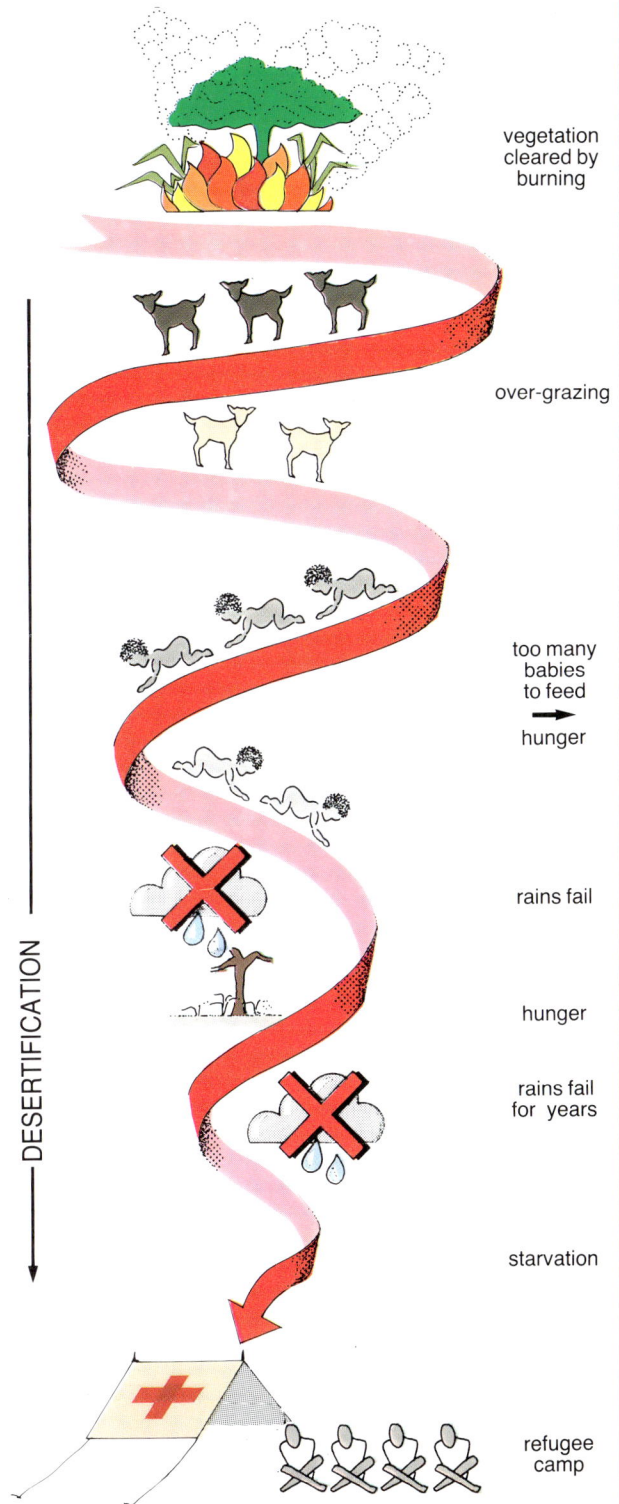

DESERTIFICATION: THE DOWNWARD SPIRAL

vegetation cleared by burning

over-grazing

too many babies to feed

→ hunger

rains fail

hunger

rains fail for years

starvation

refugee camp

DESERTIFICATION

A Refugee Camp in Chad. The people sit in long rows in the sun waiting to be fed. What do you notice about the people? Try and describe how they spend the day.

Pakistan many of the problems described above are beginning to appear. The scale of disaster there has not yet grown to an unmanageable level. But steps have to be taken **now** to halt the damaging effects of deforestation, and the damage being done by unwise use of flood irrigation.

In the Atacama, Kalahari and Australian deserts there are so few people that the effects of climatic change have not yet produced the same tragedies as in the Sahel. Elsewhere, in the USA and some Middle East countries, the wealth of the country enables modern technology to be used to reduce the suffering and loss. But **nowhere** is safe from mismanagement and misfortune. It is in the USA that the largest amount of land has been destroyed by flood irrigation.

REFUGEES: THE DOWNWARD SPIRAL

Of all the desert lands in crisis it is the Sahel in Africa that is suffering most. (See the map on page 10.) People who could once manage to live at the desert edge can no longer do so. Those who kept animals have seen their herds die, and those who grew crops have seen them fail in the drought. The removal of trees plus death of the herds means there is neither wood nor dung for fuel. One result is that what little food there is cannot be cooked properly. This encourages the spread of more diseases.

Many people have moved to refugee camps in search of food and water. Unknown numbers have become too weak to move and have died of starvation in their homelands.

Many others have died on the long march to the camps or died after they arrived. So many have died that most relief agencies have stopped counting.

The Major Problems

1 The sheer size of the disaster in Africa is almost beyond understanding. It is estimated that between fifty and sixty million people are starving in the Sahel and the desert itself. This is equal to the total population of Great Britain, or to the combined populations of the three largest cities in the USA. About one in ten of these people have already died. Some relief agencies estimate the death total will exceed ten millions by 1990.

2 In the countries most affected the lack of education, of skills and of modern technology, prevent people doing very much to help themselves.

   For example, the people are quite unable to drill deep wells for water, even when they know where to drill. Water is often brought to them by road tankers.

3 Supplies of food do not always get through to the starving. This is partly due to the state of the roads and lack of transport. (See the photograph on this page.) In several parts of Ethiopia the war is increasingly interfering with supplies.

4 There is also confusion among European and American helpers about the best ways to help. Sometimes this is due to misunderstanding the customs of the people they are trying to help.

   In one camp workers were horrified to discover that when they tried to feed the babies first the mothers ate the food. The helpers had to feed the mothers and babies separately. It is not that the mothers do not love their children. It is that when the tribe is threatened with destruction the mothers are the ones who must be cared for first. They do most of the farming and they can have more children. What help would the starving babies be in the desert? It is only in rich and secure countries that it is possible to put women **and** children first.

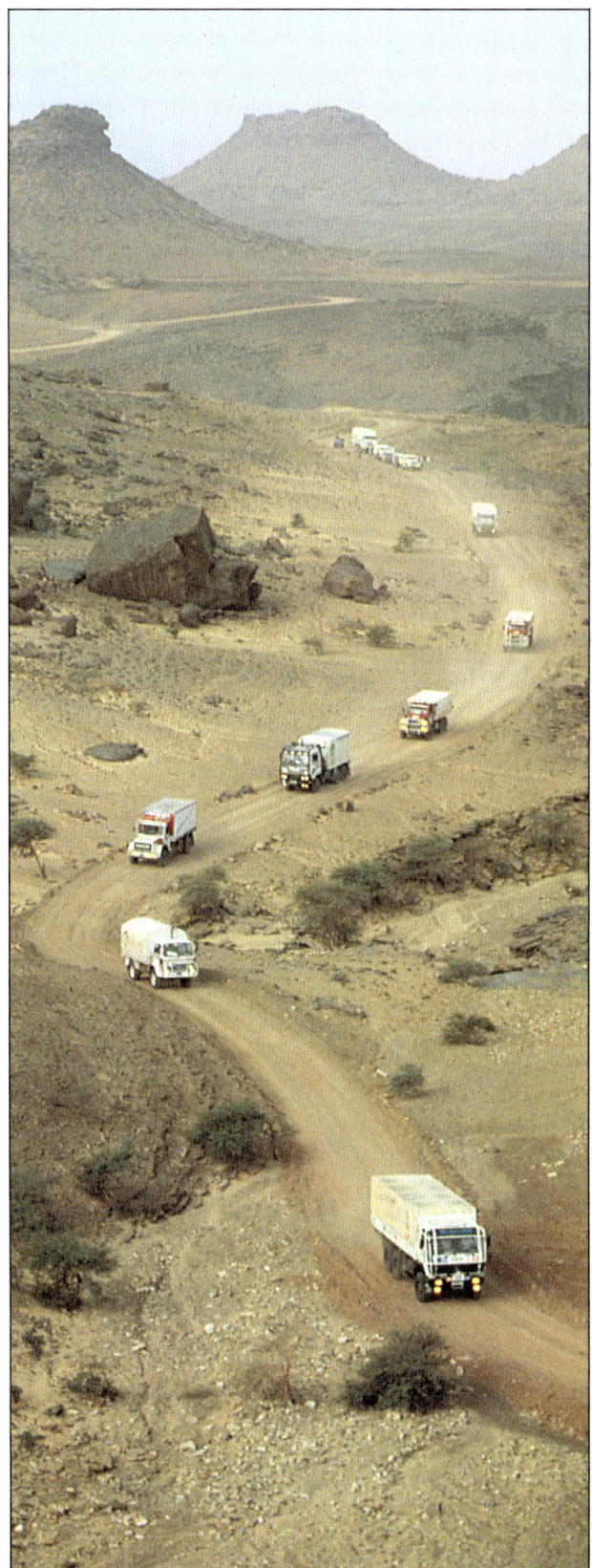

Food Convoy. This French convoy is carrying food into the Sahel in Chad. There are forty lorries altogether but several are not carrying food on this long tough haul. What are they carrying? The nature of the road and country suggest the answers.

CHAPTER FOUR

PEOPLE ADVANCE

EMERGENCY ACTION

The people of the world are trying to understand and to help with a major emergency in Africa. This emergency is likely to continue until the end of this century.

Helping with this emergency has to be our first priority.

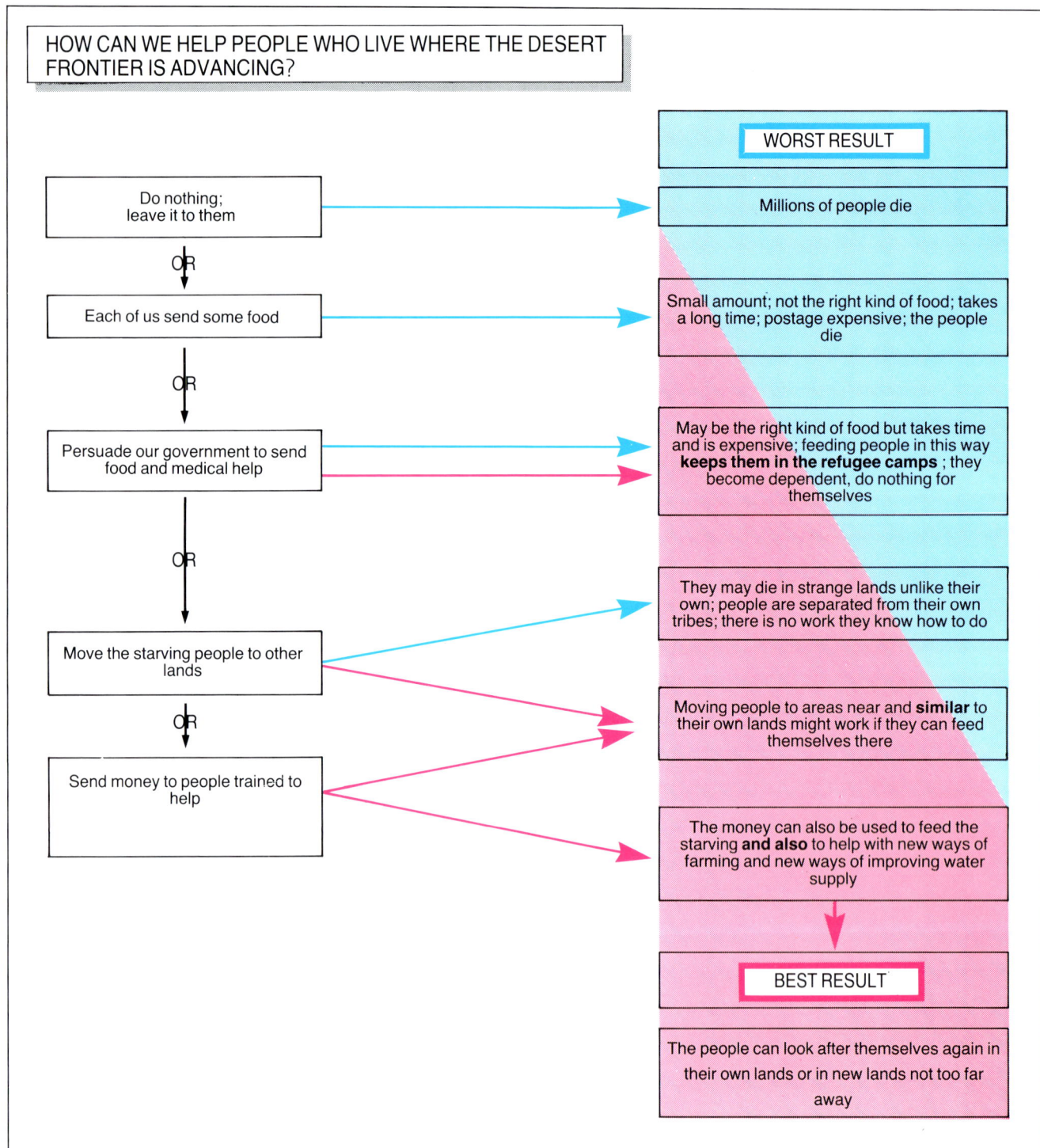

HOW CAN WE HELP PEOPLE WHO LIVE WHERE THE DESERT FRONTIER IS ADVANCING?

WORST RESULT

Do nothing; leave it to them

→ Millions of people die

OR

Each of us send some food

→ Small amount; not the right kind of food; takes a long time; postage expensive; the people die

OR

Persuade our government to send food and medical help

→ May be the right kind of food but takes time and is expensive; feeding people in this way **keeps them in the refugee camps**; they become dependent, do nothing for themselves

OR

Move the starving people to other lands

→ They may die in strange lands unlike their own; people are separated from their own tribes; there is no work they know how to do

→ Moving people to areas near and **similar** to their own lands might work if they can feed themselves there

OR

Send money to people trained to help

→ The money can also be used to feed the starving **and also** to help with new ways of farming and new ways of improving water supply

BEST RESULT

The people can look after themselves again in their own lands or in new lands not too far away

What Can We Do?

If your family spent a little less on food each week you could send that saving to people who are helping at the desert edge.

For example:

Saving a pound a week in Great Britain would mean giving up **only one** of the following for a week:

EITHER/OR

2 packets of biscuits
2 loaves of bread
4 small bars of chocolate
2 bags of sugar

A similar saving in the USA would be about 2 dollars.

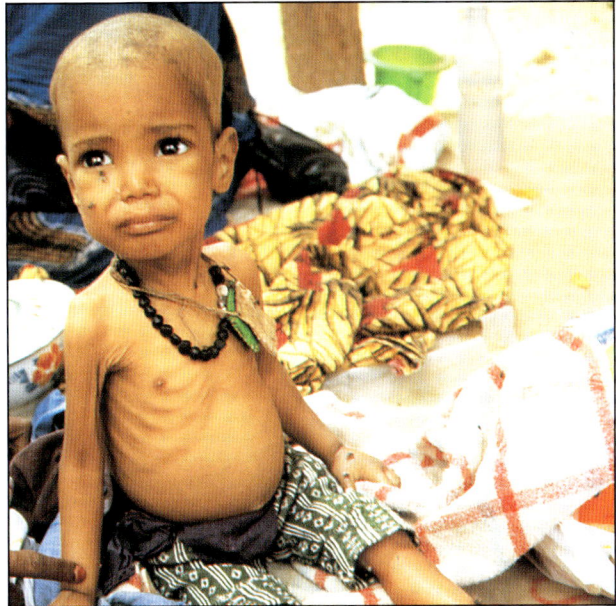

Starving in the Sahel (Mali).

WAR ON WANT
37-39 Great Guildford Street
LONDON SE1 0ES

CHRISTIAN AID
Interchurch House
35-41 Lower Marsh Road
Waterloo
LONDON SE1 7RL

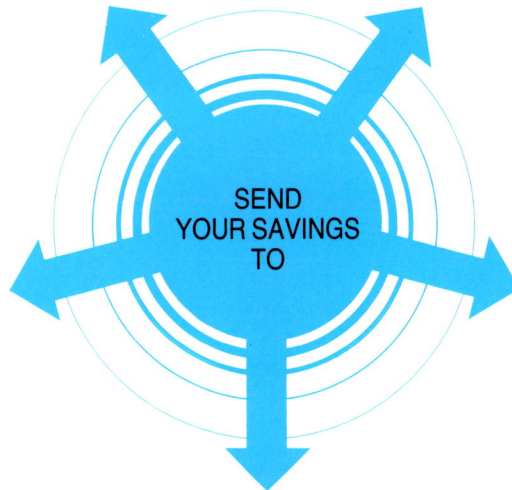

SEND
YOUR SAVINGS
TO

SAVE THE CHILDREN
Mary Datchelor House
17 Grove Lane
LONDON SE1 8RD

OXFAM
274 Banbury Road
OXFORD OX2 7DZ

THE RED CROSS
National HQ
Appeals Dept
9 Grosvenor Crescent
LONDON SW1X 7EJ

RESETTLEMENT

Emergency aid for people in the camps is vital. But long-term aid is needed to help the people out of the camps and back to supporting themselves on the land. Returning people to the land is called **resettlement.**

Resettlement of refugees is a major task confronting the whole world. It needs the resources of the whole world because the countries suffering most are too poor to tackle this huge problem. The resettlement will be partly through returning a small number of people to the least damaged parts of their homelands. But the majority may have to go to new lands.

Resettlement requires the co-operation of the people and the right kinds of help. The photograph on this page suggests that even in a wealthy country resettlement can go wrong if people are not given the right kinds of help.

The first step is to accept that large parts of the old homelands are destroyed by desertification. Most people in the camps will never return to them.

The second step is to recognize that refugees who are moved to new lands must behave in new ways:

1 They have to be integrated with the people already living there.
2 They have to take up a new lifestyle that does not encourage desertification.
3 They have to take up effective birth control. If they do not control the size of their families then the terrible truth is that famine will do it for them.

Aborigine family picking over a rubbish tip in Weipa, Queensland, Australia.

House building and nomadic houses at Diredawa, Ethiopia. This is part of a resettlement scheme for some of the Afar people who lived in the Danakil Desert. Compare this photograph with the photograph on page 18. How have their lives been changed by resettlement?

Successful Resettlement

Successful resettlement requires many things to happen. Here are some of the most important:

1 **Water supply**

Resettlement areas must not only receive enough rainfall to support life, there must be water storage facilities as well. Extra wells may need to be dug. Several areas in the Ethiopian Highlands seem suitable.

2 **Tree planting**

The number of trees has to be great enough to provide fuel, shade and prevent desertification beginning again. These trees must be established before large numbers of refugees arrive. Several kinds of quick-growing trees from Australia are being planted out in parts of the Sahel. Unfortunately, quick-growing trees take a lot of water out of the soil. Land used for these trees cannot be used for other crops as well.

3 **The free grazing of animals must stop**

For many refugees this means giving up a nomadic life and becoming settled. The photograph on this page shows a part of this process.

4 **Scarce resources such as trees and water have to be very carefully used**

The soil must be fed and cared for as though it was a crop itself.

5 **Education**

The refugees need education to avoid the mistakes of the past. Two particular areas for education are:

   a. new farming methods,
   b. birth control.

The great advance that could come from this crisis is the development of new ways of living in the deserts and at the desert edges. The lessons learned can be used in all the arid places of the world.

Key words

resettlement – settle again. This word is most often used to describe people being settled in a new land. It can **also** mean, as it does here, resettlement in old lands but in a new style; e.g. as farmers and not as nomads.

integrated – combined into a whole. In this case two or more tribal groups combining peacefully and successfully into a single community.

RECLAIMING THE DESERT

In all the deserts areas are being reclaimed and improved. More crops are being grown and more food per hectare is being produced. The largest advances into the desert are taking place in the richer countries, for example, in Algeria and Saudi Arabia. (See the photographs on pages 31 and 33.)

Big or small, all the reclaimed areas share things in common:

1 The areas reclaimed must have a reliable water supply. In poor countries this has to be a local supply from wells and springs. (See the photograph on page 23.) In richer countries some areas are fed by water piped over long distances. (See the photograph on page 36.)
2 The soils or sands have to be fixed and stabilized.
3 Reclaimed land has to be very carefully farmed. Any of the actions that might cause desertification have to be avoided.

In areas very exposed to the wind the first step in reclaiming the sands is to fix the dunes in position by planting grasses. If this is not done any other plants put into the sand will be buried and suffocated in a few hours.

The second step is shown in the photograph on this page. The men are planting shelter belts of plants which will anchor the sand, reduce wind damage and make it possible to plant out tree seedlings. The plant being used here is a Euphorbia. It can root itself in sand and survive on very little water. If tree seedlings were planted without growing this protection first they would all be smothered by the sand. In areas likely to be shared between animals and crops the shelter-belt plants will be extremely thorny shrubs which are known to keep out even the greediest goat. (See the photograph on page 15.)

In some of the oil-rich countries of the Middle East other methods of fixing the sand are used. For example, dunes are sprayed with an oil product from the refinery and this fixes the sand. It also helps to hold the moisture in the sand. Grasses and seedlings can then be planted out. This expensive

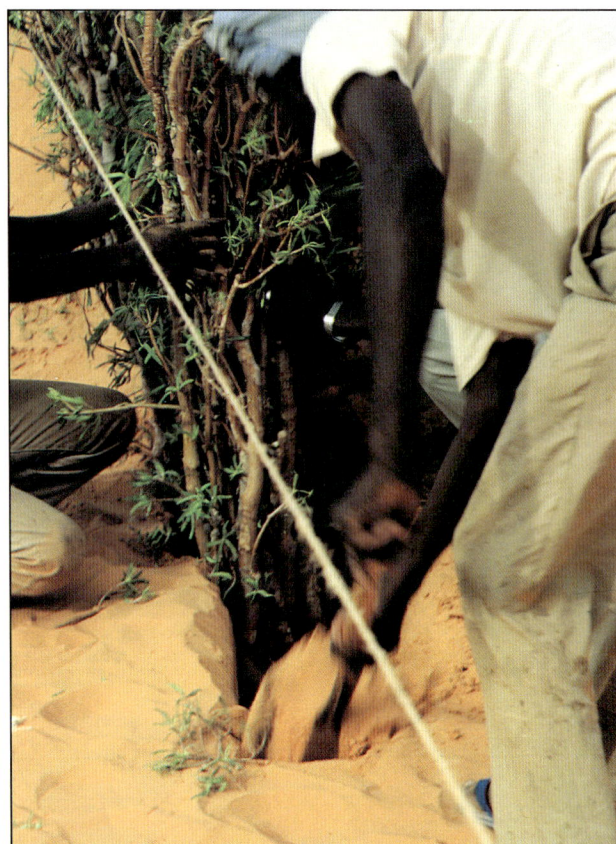

Advance into the desert in Mauritania. Here men are planting Euphorbia in shelter belts before tree planting can begin.

method is not available in most countries.

The large photograph on page 31 shows a big area of fixed dunes in Algeria. This is a good example of **the frontier** in the battle between people and desert.

The dunes have to be fixed to stop them advancing into the area of trees and farmland. Now the dunes are fixed the farmers can advance into them by tree planting, and by improving the sands until crops can be grown.

Once enclosures with trees are well established many other crops can be grown. These may include beans, clover, grains, fruits and dates. All these plants become sources of **humus** for the soil. To avoid exhausting the soil a different crop may be grown in the same enclosure each year. This system is called crop rotation. In areas where food for people and animals is plentiful some crops may be ploughed directly into the soil to enrich it. Clover is sometimes used in this way.

Fixed dunes in Algeria. At the desert edge in Algeria moving dunes have been stabilized by planting grasses and trees on the dunes. The shapes of the dunes are clearly shown by the lines of plants.

Key words

reclaim – win back from a waste condition.
fixed – secured in place – dunes will not move.
stabilized – dunes will not change shape.
humus – vegetable and plant material in the soil.

FARMING IN THE DESERT

The two main types of farming in the deserts are **settled farming** and **nomadic farming.**

Settled farming is mainly growing crops. Nomadic farming is mainly concerned with grazing animals. The types of farming can be shown very simply in this diagram.

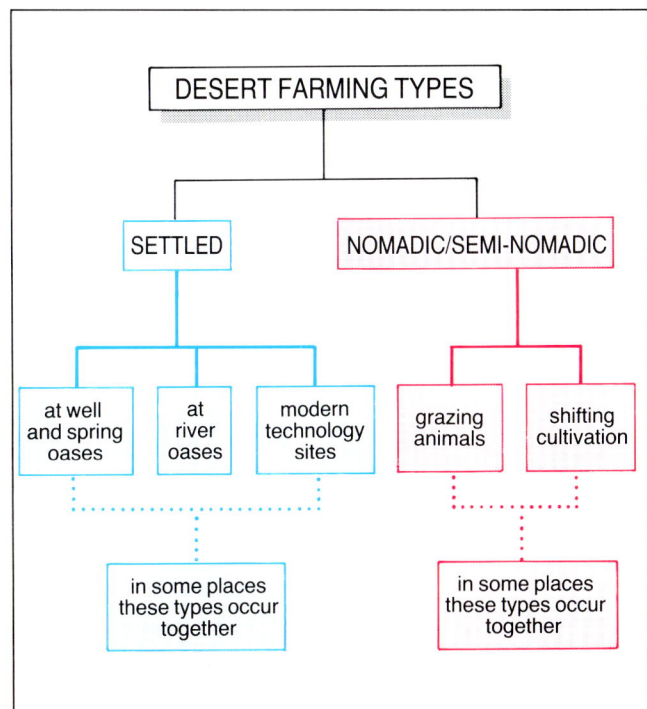

DESERT FARMING TYPES

SETTLED

NOMADIC/SEMI-NOMADIC

at well and spring oases

at river oases

modern technology sites

grazing animals

shifting cultivation

in some places these types occur together

in some places these types occur together

Settled Farming

The oasis in the photograph on page 4 is long-established and includes many trees,

The Edge of the Desert. This is the Hotan Oasis, Xinjiang Province, China. It shows very clearly the wheat fields with their shelter belts. It also shows the sharp line of the frontier between cropland and desert.

Advance into the desert at Bilma, Niger.

especially date palms. A newer development like the one at Bilma (see photograph on this page) looks very different. The newest enclosures do not have trees.

Although the date palm is very important a long-established oasis will have many other crops. These include olives, lemons, figs, apricots, guavas, tomatoes and spices. At the larger oases like that at Hotan (see photograph on this page) wheat, millet, beans, peas and sweet potatoes may be grown.

Oases are often important as watering places for nomads and travellers in the desert. If the nomads are moving herds of cattle, sheep or goats then the croplands of the oasis will be protected by a strong fence or thick thorn hedge. The animals will be watered outside this area. The water will be run along a pipe or ditch to the animals.

A river oasis may be very large. For example, at the River Nile in Egypt the croplands occupy a very long strip of country on each side of the river. Field crops are very much more important here, including maize, millet, wheat and beans. Close to the Nile large areas are used for rice. Cairo and Alexandria get much of their food from the Nile Valley. Some is exported to other countries.

There are **three** features that link all these oases:

1 Some crops can be grown more than once a year because of the favourable combination of high temperatures and irrigation water. This is known as double cropping. If the soil is cared for and fertilized double cropping does not cause the bad effects of overcropping.

2 Much of the work is still done by traditional methods. For example, the method of raising water shown on page 42.

Rotary Irrigation and its effect on the landscape. This machine is a clever development from the ordinary rotating lawn sprinkler. It is driven on a circular course and creates a circle of cropland.

3 At all oases animals are kept under strict control. This applies if they belong to the local farmers just as much as if they are driven there by nomadic herdsmen.

At the largest oases where there is plenty of water and modern farming methods are used the croplands are being pushed into the desert. The photograph of the oasis at Hotan, China (page 32), shows this situation.

In the richest of the desert countries the use of modern methods can change the scenery dramatically. Places where this happens can be called modern technology sites. The photographs on this page are excellent examples of this kind of farming. In the oil-rich or westernized states of the Middle East money and technology are changing the face of the desert.

Nomadic Farming

Farming at many oases is pushing back the desert frontier but the nomadic way of life is declining. Herdsmen are seen as encouraging the spread of desert by allowing their herds to roam from one overgrazed pasture to another. Their life is becoming poorer and more restricted. For example, many herdsmen in the Sahel who once drove cattle along the desert edge, found it necessary to herd sheep and goats instead. Today, pastures are

so poor only goats and camels can survive. In other countries, for example, in parts of Jordan, large areas of the desert are being fenced off from animals.

By the end of this century it may be that the only nomads still living in desert lands will be those who are traders. They will still be travelling with salt, dates, metal wares, carpets and spices from one oasis to another. And no one will be eating very much meat.

The semi-nomadic life based on shifting cultivation is also failing. This way of life will be very restricted in the next few years.

QUESTIONS TO CONSIDER

Look through this book at all the photographs of farming and irrigation. Now answer the following question.

Explain which kinds of farming would be most affected by:
1 rapid movements of nearby sand-dunes
2 shortages of fuel oil
3 the invention of very cheap water-pumps worked by sunlight
4 severe drought
5 breakdown of machinery
6 rapid spread of diseases affecting people
7 famine

CHAPTER FIVE

THE FUTURE FOR PEOPLE IN THE DESERTS

HOW MANY PEOPLE?

A desert land can easily become overpopulated. Much of the Atacama Desert in South America has a population density of less than 1 person per square kilometre. Even a small increase in population to 3 persons per square kilometre would turn parts of the Atacama into a disaster area like parts of the Sudan and Ethiopia.

Two of the main reasons why populations are increasing in desert lands are:
1 Improvements in health mean that more babies will live to become adults. They will have children of their own.
2 In the years of enough rainfall and good crops people increase the size of their families. Worse still, nomadic people will be attracted into the area by the better pastures. Both the human and animal populations are increased.

Unfortunately, this population increase occurs mainly among people who are very poor. Their income each year is less than £100 (about $200) per person. Even in the good years they have no wealth to spend on new roads, modern wells or warehouses for storing food.

When desertification begins the population is decreased almost at once by drought, famine and disease. This tragic, repeated pattern has to be stopped.

A number of wise observers, including HRH Prince Philip, Duke of Edinburgh, have pointed to the valuable idea of **optimum populations.**

An optimum population in a desert would be the population **small enough** to:
1 survive through the worst years,
2 not cause desertification in any years, including the best years.

This can apply just as well to animals as to people.

There are two main actions to be taken if this idea is to work. First, there must be widespread use of birth control so the population decreases in numbers. Second, many of the nomadic peoples have to become settled in homelands of their own.

In some deserts, including the Sahara and Thar, a third action will be needed. In areas already overpopulated some of the people will have to agree to be resettled elsewhere.

If these plans could be carried out then desert peoples would know that their homelands could support them. They could take charge of their future instead of being victims of disaster.

There are many reasons why this valuable idea of optimum population is not being used throughout the desert lands. But the main reason is **ignorance.**

Many of the people have little education. For example, in Ethiopia, only 32 per cent of children go to Primary Schools, only 12 per cent go to Secondary Schools. In some rural areas no one goes to school at all. No one can read instructions on a food packet or on a bottle of medicine.

Many of the people trying to help are also ignorant. For example, the first census in Ethiopia was not held until 1984. The population was discovered to be 8 millions more than the biggest official estimate. This mistake, which is nearly 25 per cent of the whole population, made a complete nonsense of all the planning for aid and development. It is also important to remember that most of those 8 million people are the poor people of the country. The problem would not be so serious if millions of wealthy and educated people had been left out.

In most of the desert countries there is a **lack of reliable information.** Not enough is known about rainfall records, about soils, about all the information useful in planning.

Artificial Water Hole, Jordan. A development like this is seen as a good idea by the tribesmen and by the camels. But what will happen if this encourages the tribesmen to have more children and the camels to have more baby camels? New modern water holes can only be useful if they are part of a proper development plan. That plan needs to be based on knowing the optimum population for the area.

There is a lack of communications of all kinds. There is a shortage of good roads, railways, television, books and newspapers.

One result of ignorance is that some aid programmes fail. They are based on incorrect information. In other cases western ideas of what will be helpful are wrong. For example, it has been estimated that since 1970 over half the irrigation schemes started in Africa, with western aid, have already failed. (See page 36.)

In some desert lands people have been cleared off the land to make way for large-scale farming schemes, for example, growing more cotton in the Sudan. This is exported and increases the wealth of the country. But little of that wealth reaches the poor peasants now starving because they have lost their land. The state is richer, the people are poorer.

The way forward chosen by some desert peoples is war. Attempts are being made to overthrow governments in several desert lands. This increases the suffering of all the people.

In the end the only way forward will be to answer the question: **how many people?** If desert people are not helped to answer this question then famine and disease will answer it for them.

WATER MANAGEMENT

The photographs on this page and the facing page show the great differences between kinds of water management.

The black and white photograph shows a local scheme which is cheap. It is worked by the local people themselves.

The colour photograph is of an advanced technology site producing water by a very expensive and complicated method.

Other examples of water use and management are shown on pages 23, 32, 33 and 35.

Water management is about using scarce water efficiently for people, their animals and crops. Here are some examples.

Drinking water for people must be pure. Whenever local inhabitants at an oasis are taught simple ways of purifying the water there is an immediate improvement in their health.

In many places modern wells are being sunk. New cheap plastic piping and storage tanks are being used. This has to be managed carefully. If too many deep wells are sunk they may draw off all the underground water. It is also clear that too many wells might also encourage desertification. Water plans must be linked with population plans.

Irrigation schemes are also a part of water management. Unfortunately, a number of new schemes have failed. They have been too expensive and too complicated for local farmers to operate. In some parts of the Sahel farmers have abandoned new schemes and now concentrate on the less reliable rain-fed crops which they know how to grow.

The most serious failures have been of flood irrigation where water is poured directly onto the land. (See the photograph on page 17.) Repeated flooding under the hot sun has caused most of the water to be lost by evaporation. All the salts in the water have stayed in the soils and ruined them. It is estimated that 80 per cent of the flood irrigated lands in the USA will soon be destroyed.

Once again crisis is both danger and opportunity.

From these failures has developed the science of hydroponics. Hydroponics is concerned with methods of feeding water direct-

Desalination Plant, Farasan Island, Saudi Arabia. The production of fresh water from sea water is a very expensive process.

ly to plants. The ground is not flooded first. One example is feeding water and liquid fertilizer directly to plant roots. This can be done by burying plastic hosepipes under the sand and pumping carefully measured amounts of water to the plants. The hoses have many tiny holes in them to let the water escape to the plants. A second example is the invention of tiny grains of a new plastic. These grains swell up to several times their size as they soak up the water. They can be mixed in below the soil surface when crop planting takes place. Irrigation water is held against the roots of plants and not lost by evaporation at the soil surface.

As new methods become more widely available and cheaper, poor farmers will be able to use them. Water management will become more efficient for the poor as well as the rich.

Water Harvesting. This is a water-harvesting scheme at Rom, near Ouahigouya, Burkina Faso. The local people are building curved walls of stones. These low walls slow the speed of rainwater running off the land. This holds moisture in the soil and checks soil erosion.

SUN POWER

Life in deserts is dominated by the sun. This is another example of danger and opportunity for desert people.

Dangers include the burning, drying, destroying effects of the sun. Water is evaporated before it reaches the crops. Soils are baked dry and made friable ready for attack by the wind. People and animals living in deserts require more water for life than they would in a cooler climate.

The opportunity is that sunlight is power. If this power is used properly it can improve the lives of desert peoples.

The photograph on this page is of solar panels. These panels use the power of the sun to heat water. This is the best known way of using sun power. Other ways are being developed.

Solar Panels, Baja California, Mexico. These panels use sunlight to heat water.

SUN POWER · 1 ·

1. Concentrating The Power Of The Sun: some different examples

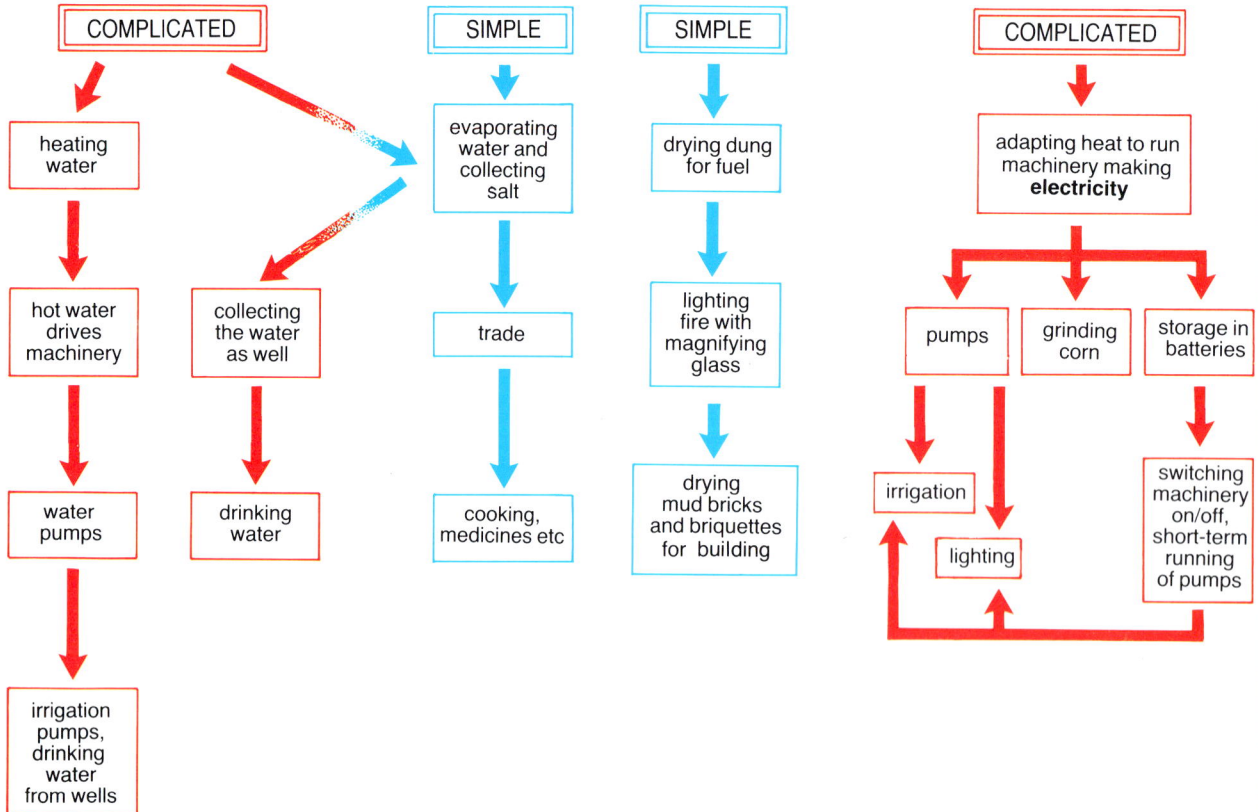

COMPLICATED
- heating water
  - hot water drives machinery
    - water pumps
      - irrigation pumps, drinking water from wells
  - collecting the water as well
    - drinking water

SIMPLE
- evaporating water and collecting salt
  - trade
    - cooking, medicines etc

SIMPLE
- drying dung for fuel
  - lighting fire with magnifying glass
    - drying mud bricks and briquettes for building

COMPLICATED
- adapting heat to run machinery making **electricity**
  - pumps
    - irrigation
  - grinding corn
    - lighting
  - storage in batteries
    - switching machinery on/off, short-term running of pumps

N.B. Sun power can be part of water management

THE FUTURE FOR PEOPLE IN DESERTS

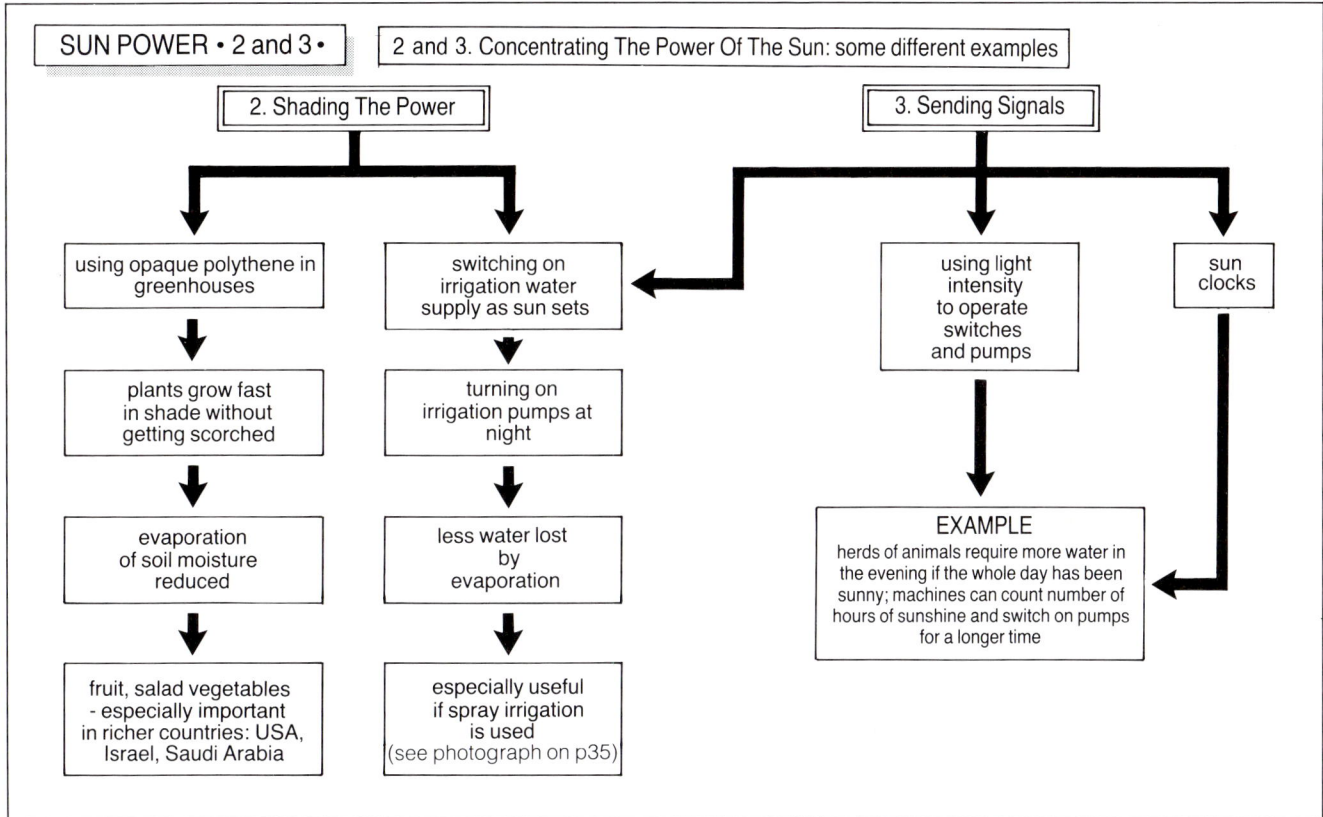

SUN POWER • 2 and 3 • | 2 and 3. Concentrating The Power Of The Sun: some different examples

2. Shading The Power

- using opaque polythene in greenhouses
  - → plants grow fast in shade without getting scorched
    - → evaporation of soil moisture reduced
      - → fruit, salad vegetables - especially important in richer countries: USA, Israel, Saudi Arabia

- switching on irrigation water supply as sun sets
  - → turning on irrigation pumps at night
    - → less water lost by evaporation
      - → especially useful if spray irrigation is used (see photograph on p35)

3. Sending Signals

- using light intensity to operate switches and pumps
- sun clocks

EXAMPLE
herds of animals require more water in the evening if the whole day has been sunny; machines can count number of hours of sunshine and switch on pumps for a longer time

The power of the sun can be used in three main ways:

1 concentrating the power
2 shading the power
3 sending signals.

All these ideas and others are being explored. The danger is that because these ideas are expensive when first developed they might remain in the hands of the rich countries and the rich landowners. The opportunity is that aid from abroad could be used to produce small, cheap power units to suit all needs.

Large desalination plants (see the photograph on page 36) could be run entirely on sun power. But these large units will always be coastal and government owned. However, most of the other ideas can be developed as small, cheap units. For example, many oases can increase food production with small polythene greenhouses. Water can be pumped into them by sun-powered heat pumps. Some of these ideas are already in operation. Many more will be by the year 2000.

Diesel Water Pump, Nile Valley, Egypt. This portable pump is being used to raise extra water out of the main irrigation ditch. If it was operated by sun power it would be much lighter to move and cheaper to run.
What would be the other advantages?
This picture of a diesel pump could give you an idea for a funny story. If it does then enter the competition. A small prize will be given by the author to the writer of the funniest story. The story must include the words:
'it would never have happened if we had had a sun pump'. State your name, address and age when sending your entry to the publishers.

39

TOURISM AND MINING

Relying on foreign aid is not the way forward for desert peoples. There are two main reasons for this:

1 Some of the aid is in the form of loans. These have to be repaid.
2 Much of the aid is as gifts. This aid could stop at any time. For example, the USA is by far the most generous country in giving aid. But because the American standard of living is so high and so expensive the country is becoming deeply in debt to the rest of the world. How much longer can the USA afford to be so generous with aid to others?

In the long term it is important that desert peoples earn the money they need for their own future plans. The main ways of earning money are by:

1 farm exports, e.g. cotton, fruits
2 earnings from tourists
3 mining exports, e.g. oil, gold, potash

Some of the dangers and opportunities facing farmers have been discussed in chapters 3 and 4, and earlier in this chapter. If the land is better cared for, the water resources better managed, then farm exports might increase.

Tourism

There are three main attractions for tourists in the desert:

1 The sunshine.
   This is especially enjoyed at coastal and oasis resorts in North Africa, Israel and parts of the Middle East. In the USA many wealthy people retire to luxury homes in the desert, for example, at Phoenix, Arizona.
2 The scenery.
   Tourists want to see exciting scenery. They go to places like the Painted Desert, USA, the Pinnacles Desert, Australia or Ayres Rock, Australia.
3 Ancient sites.
   Sites such as the pyramids in the Nile Valley, Egypt attract many tourists. But other desert lands offer similar attractions, e.g. in Israel, Jordan and Syria.

Very few tourists are willing to live 'rough', particularly in country as dangerous

Swimming Pool, Hotel Saharien, Douz, Tunisia.

Potash Works at the Dead Sea, Israel.

as desert. If the tourist industry is to expand and bring in wealth then new airports, roads, hotels and good supplies of water have to be provided. Local people have to be trained to work in hotels and restaurants.

Compare the photograph of the tourist hotel with the photographs of oases on pages 4, 32 and 35. In what ways is a tourist centre rather like an oasis? What is it that is 'produced' at tourist centres?

Mining

The photograph on this page is of a mining centre. In what ways is a mine like an oasis? How is it different?

Successful oases and tourist centres can go on growing and improving. They are a permanent asset to the country. But a mine has a limited life. Once all the oil, gold or iron has been mined it closes.

Income from mining has a short life. Even the huge oil incomes of some Middle East states will soon come to an end. This income has to be invested now to protect the future of these countries. Communications must be improved. Schools, colleges, hospitals and good housing must be built. Some of the money needs to be spent on improving farming and tourism.

The danger is that oil incomes will be wasted on luxuries for the few rich people. The opportunity is that the money may be spent in ways that improve the future for all the peoples in the desert lands.

CONCLUSIONS

The main theme in this book has been that every crisis in the desert lands presents the people with both danger and opportunity. There are many examples of how desert peoples can use both their own skills and foreign aid to turn crisis from danger to opportunity. But if the deserts are really to be defeated then it is important to avoid crises starting in the first place.

The first step to avoid crises is to recognize that the centres of most deserts will never be turned into farmlands. Except at oases, tourist centres and mines most of the deserts

A Persian Wheel lifting water from the Indus River, Pakistan. This wheel, named after the country where is was invented, has been in use for thousands of years. It is a vital piece of equipment for many peasant farmers. To replace it by some other method might upset the balance between the people and their environment.

will remain unchanged. The photographs on pages 11 and 12 show clearly why this is so.

The second step in avoiding crises is to recognize that overpopulation is destroying the way of life. At the desert edge, and at river and well oases, the people are suffering. The main reason is that the population has increased to the point where the land can no longer support it **even in the good years.** In periods of drought the situation is far worse.

At the moment overpopulation is being corrected by famine and death. This tragedy is most marked in the Sahel. But in nearly all the desert lands it is estimated that one person in three is starving. One person in ten will die of starvation or related diseases.

Huge amounts of foreign aid are being poured into emergency relief work. But the danger is that people are being kept alive in camps only to return to their old ways on land already exhausted by years of overcropping and overgrazing.

If the central problem of overpopulation is not dealt with through birth control the situation can only get worse.

Crises have also come to the desert peoples because they have not understood they are part of a delicately balanced environment. As long as there were trees to cut down people cut them down. As in the western world little thought was given to replanting. Now there is neither fuel, building materials nor shelter for many people. And the soils are being blown away even faster than in the past.

The desert peoples have to learn the same lesson as everyone else. The world can only support us if we care for the world.

The world can be cared for by local efforts helped by international co-operation.

An outstanding example of this has been the use of stone lines in Burkina Faso. This is shown on page 37. Local stones are collected

Land reclamation, United Arab Emirates. Here in the UAE modern methods and materials are being used to water trees in a land reclamation scheme. Carefully controlled amounts of water are pumped along perforated hosepipes feeding water directly to each tree.

and placed in curving lines like small contour lines across the slopes. These lines hold up the run-off of rainwater. They are like small terraces. This keeps the soil moist and reduces soil erosion. Crop yields have increased by 50 per cent. The soil level has risen as much as 150mm in the fields with stone lines. It has fallen 100mm in the fields without lines. This successful scheme developed with help from Oxfam shows what is needed for success in many desert places.

1 **The local people operate the scheme.**
2 **It is extremely cheap and easily learned.**
3 **It does not depend on continuous overseas aid but on people helping themselves.**

If aid of the wrong kind is given this may do as much harm as severe drought. It is especially important that the rich desert states help the poorer. They have a better understanding of the situation than many western states.

In many cases changes need to be small. For example, if flood irrigation cannot be changed to another type then an improvement can be made by opening the flood gates only at night. In other places there are opportunities for bigger changes. These include the use of hydroponics and other newer water management methods. And in the future sun power will be harnessed for use in the deserts.

As each new opportunity for improving life is taken up we know there is a new crisis waiting. If better crops are used for feeding even more babies then the refugee camps will always be full. There are several causes of desertification but overpopulation is one of the most serious. It is also a cause that could be controlled by the desert peoples themselves.

GLOSSARY

Deforestation – clearing forest from the land.

Desertification – the spread of desert conditions.

Ephemeral – lasting a few days only. Used to describe plants with a short life cycle.

Erg – African name for a sand sea desert.

Evaporation – the process by which water is changed into water vapour.

Hamada – African name for bare rock desert.

Hydroponics – irrigation by feeding measured quantities of water directly to individual plants. (Water is saved by reducing effects of evaporation.)

Irrigation – watering the land by artificial means, e.g. spray irrigation.

Oasis – a place in the desert where water is regularly available.

Optimum population – the population which is appropriate to the resources of an environment.

Overgrazing – too many animals for the environment to support. The result is destruction of the grasslands.

Overpopulation – too many people or animals for the environment to support.

Population – the number of people or animals living in a place.

Reg – African name for a stony desert.

Sahel – The belt of dry lands at the south edge of the Sahara Desert.

Wadi – desert watercourse which is usually dry. A wadi may flood very rapidly during heavy rains.

Xerophyte – drought resistant plants, e.g. cactus.

FURTHER READING

Carson, J. *Deserts and People* Wayland 1982

Cloudsley-Thompson, J. *The Desert* Orbis 1974

Cloudsley-Thompson, J. *Desert Life* Aldus Books 1975

Goldsmith, E and Hildyard, N. (Ed.) *The Earth Report* Mitchell Beazley 1988

Grainger, A. *Desertification* Earthscan 1982

Lye, K. (Ed.) *Encyclopaedia of Africa* Macdonald Education 1976

Monahan, Patricia *Deserts* Macdonald Education 1983

National Geographic Society *Desert Realm* 1982

Steyn, H. P. *Bushmen of the Kalahari* Wayland 1985

Tyler, Margaret *Desert* Hart-Davis 1974